CONTENTS

- 6 — Official guide to Vlogging
- 8 — Alfie Deyes
- 10 — Zoella
- 12 — Wordsearch
- 14 — Louise Pentland
- 16 — The EPIC Vlogger quiz
- 18 — Marcus Butler
- 20 — Spot the difference
- 22 — Jim Chapman
- 24 — Tanya Burr
- 26 — Educational Fun
- 28 — Fun for Louis
- 30 — Carrie Hope Fletcher
- 32 — Match the Vlogger
- 34 — Tom Fletcher
- 36 — Spot the Vlogger
- 38 — Rise of the Beauty Vloggers
- 40 — PewDiePie
- 42 — The Gamers

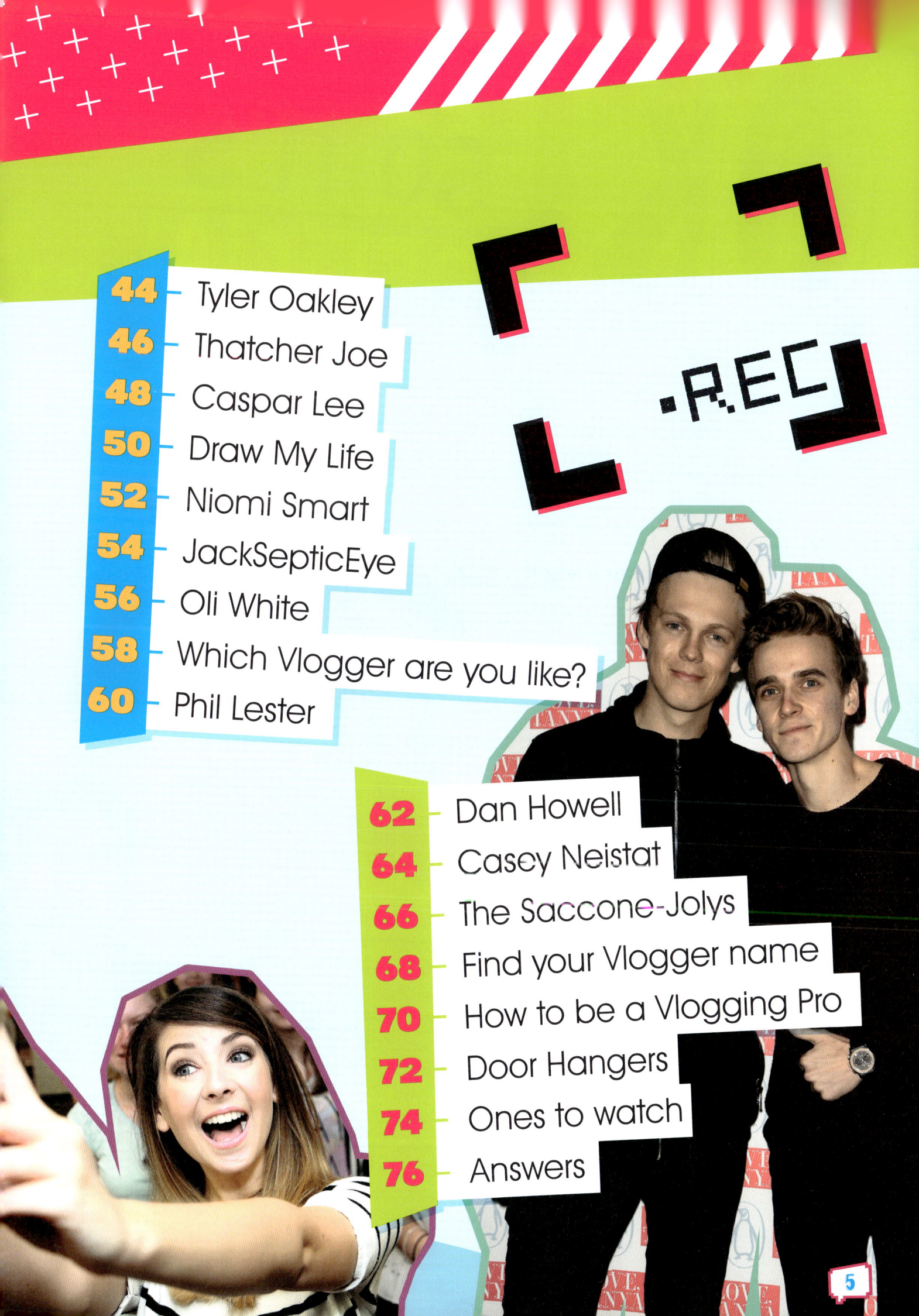

- 44 – Tyler Oakley
- 46 – Thatcher Joe
- 48 – Caspar Lee
- 50 – Draw My Life
- 52 – Niomi Smart
- 54 – JackSepticEye
- 56 – Oli White
- 58 – Which Vlogger are you like?
- 60 – Phil Lester
- 62 – Dan Howell
- 64 – Casey Neistat
- 66 – The Saccone-Jolys
- 68 – Find your Vlogger name
- 70 – How to be a Vlogging Pro
- 72 – Door Hangers
- 74 – Ones to watch
- 76 – Answers

OK, so it's OFFiCiAL...

The world has gone vlogging mad. There's always someone new and fresh on the scene to check out and it's definitely all about the vloggers these days.

#TeamInternet is growing stronger than ever and it's time to meet the epic new wave of YouTube stars becoming overnight celeb sensations.

So what is Vlogging?

If you've never heard of vloggers before then here's the low-down.

A Vlog is the name for a personal video update or online diary documenting part of your life. 'Vloggers' upload regular content on the video sharing platform YouTube where it can be watched by millions of people across the world at any time. Most vloggers have regular upload days when fans can catch up with their latest gossip. It's totally like tuning in to regular episodes of your favourite TV show or catching up with your bestie!

Different Types of Vloggers:

Vloggers all like to talk about different things and the most successful have built up a loyal fan base. They share their passions, their achievements and sometimes even their mistakes. Here are a few of the different types of vloggers you might stumble across. What are your favourite vlogger categories? Jot them into the box below.

TRAVEL VLOGGERS
These guys are always stepping out of their comfort zone and exploring new places around the world. Watch them explore and have their own crazy adventures, we feel as though we are right there with them during the highs and lows!

CHATTY VLOGGERS
They film personal moments from their life and take their camera wherever they go. They aren't afraid to film in the middle of a crowded street and talk to you through the camera just as though you're right there with them!

THE ENTERTAINERS
Actors, singers and performers of all kinds can be found hanging out on YouTube. From covering the latest chart tracks to writing or directing movies, this confident crowd are totally at home both behind and in front of the camera

EDUCATIONAL VLOGGERS
They show that learning doesn't have to be a yawn fest. Teaching you fun facts or making exciting videos based on historic events or scientific topics comes naturally to these vloggers and there's never a dull moment.

BEAUTY VLOGGERS
Got your eye on a hot product or a cute make-up brand? The beauty vloggers are the first to get their hands on the stuff we've all been dreaming about owning!

THE GAMERS
The most successful gaming vloggers chat and interact with their viewers as they play their way through the games we've all been talking about.

What are your FAVOURITE VLOGGER categories?

7

Alfie Deyes
VLOGGING PRO!

WOW! "I starred in the music video for Band Aid 30"

RECORD BREAKER He's won Guinness world records for 'most bangles put on in 30 seconds by a team of two' and 'most party poppers popped in 30 seconds' it's only a matter of time before he racks up some more!

DOB: 17/09/1993
Siblings: One sister called Poppy.
Pets: A seriously cute black pug called Nala.
Likes: Hanging out with his family and friends.
Dislikes: Rude or unkind people.
Single or Taken? Taken – he's currently dating and living with fellow YouTuber Zoe Sugg.

@PointlessBlog
@PointlessBlog
/PointlessBlogTV
PointlessBlog

BIO

At just 15 years old he decided that he would start making videos on YouTube for fun in his spare time. Little did he know that what started off as a hobby would soon go on to make him one of the biggest and most successful vloggers ever!

Alfie's videos are super chatty, fun and down to earth. He's the kind of guy who always makes time for his fans and he regularly stops to say hello and to take a picture with them out in the street. He has his own successful merchandise line and loves to create and design new products for his fans to wear and use.

Based in the seaside resort of Brighton in the UK, Alfie lives with his girlfriend and fellow vlogger Zoe Sugg - aka Zoella. They share their home with two pet guinea pigs called Percy and Pippin and their dog Nala. Their house has been dubbed the 'Zalfie Pad' by Zoe, Alfie and their fans.

Alfie Deyes is one of the most successful British vloggers of all time. With more exciting new projects being announced every week, he always has something up his sleeve to keep his fans entertained and that's why we love him!

3 of the best

Ariana Grande Does My Makeup

CHECK IT OUT

PointlessBlog Vs Zoella

CHECK IT OUT

Trying American Candy

CHECK IT OUT

MADAME TUSSAUDS

Want to strike a pose with Alfie? Well now you can. He's been forever immortalised in wax at the top London tourist attraction Madame Tussauds.

WEIRD TALENT ALERT!
Alfie can do a Rubik's cube in 30 seconds flat.

CELEB BFF
JAMIE OLIVER
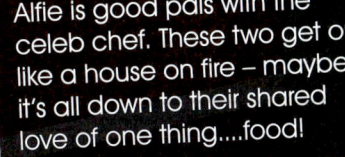
Alfie is good pals with the celeb chef. These two get on like a house on fire – maybe it's all down to their shared love of one thing....food!

CELEB CRUSH
EMMA WATSON

Okay so we all know that He's totally loved up with Zoella, but Alfie has also been very vocal about the fact that he's currently crushin' on Emma Watson. It's alright Alf – she's a total babe. We get it!

YouTube channels

Main Channel – PointlessBlog
This is Alfie's main channel where he posts his best video content. He has over 5 million subscribers.

Vlogging Channel – PointlessBlogVlogs
This is where Alfie uploads his vlogs and his more chatty content. He has over 3 million subscribers here.

Gaming Channel – PointlessBlogGames
Alfie also has his own gaming channel. He has over 1.5 million subscribers here and plays a mix of popular games.

Zoella

SUPERSTAR VLOGGER

I'M A WIZARD!
"Well, sort of. Did you know I was cast as an extra in Harry Potter and the Philosopher's Stone when I was just 10 years old?

JUST SAY YES!
Zoe suffers from anxiety but tries not to let it hold her back too much. One of her mottos in life is "Just say yes!" and she's even a digital ambassador for the mental health charity MIND.

Name: Zoe Elizabeth Sugg
DOB: 28/03/1990
Siblings: Zoe has one brother called Joe aka fellow YouTuber Thatcher Joe!
Pets: Two adorably fluffy guinea pigs called Pippin and Percy.
Likes: Spending quality time with her friends and having a giggle at totally random things!
Dislikes: Seeing people upset.
Single or Taken? Taken – she's currently dating and living with fellow YouTuber Alfie Deyes...

 @Zoella
 @Zoella
 /zoe.zoella
 officialzoella

3 of the best

BIO

Zoe Sugg grew up in Lacock, Wiltshire. After working as an apprentice interior designer (see - she's always been totally creative!) Zoe took up blogging in her spare time. Starting her own online blog and seeing how much fun it was, she quickly moved on to filming her videos and started uploading them onto YouTube in 2009 under the name Zoella.

Pretty soon we were hooked on all things Zoella! With her down-to-earth personality, she's like the best friend we all want to hang out with. She's not afraid to make fun of herself and go a little crazy sometimes, and that's what makes her the ultimate vlogging superstar.

She's bagged herself the hottest guy on the block – the one and only Mr Alfie Deyes of course. The two live in their Brighton based 'Zalfie pad' and this cute couple give us all the feels! #relationshipgoals

She's launched her own successful book series, an epic beauty line and always has a new project planned. The only way is UP for this girl, so make sure you're following along for the next chapter of her journey!

Draw My Life
CHECK IT OUT

My Everyday Make-up Routine
CHECK IT OUT

Best Friend VS Boyfriend
CHECK IT OUT

KITCHEN QUEEN!

Zoe loves to bake and is always cooking up yummy treats in her daily vlogs. She's even appeared on The Great British Bake Off for Comic Relief. A great way to combine her love of baking and helping charities in the process. Go, Zoe!

FUSSY EATER
Zoe is a self-confessed fussy eater! Don't offer her mushrooms, she HATES them. Zoe's fave foods include: Pizza, Mashed Potato and her Dad's roast dinners. We hear that the legendary Daddy Sugg makes a mean Sunday lunch!

CELEB BFFS

THE VAMPS
Zoe has met and presented with the lads from brit boy-band The Vamps a few times now and they always seem super happy to see each other.

YouTube channels

Main Channel – Zoella
Zoe's main channel where she posts her regular videos. Beauty and baking are firm faves here! Zoella has over 10,430,271 subscribers. That's seriously impressive!

Second Channel – MoreZoella
This is where you'll find Zoe hanging out on vlogs and being a lot more chilled out. She's always taking time out with her vlogging besties and her fun and friendly personality shines through.

D	Z	A	X	H	N	M	S	Y	T	C	Q	A	U	M	M	J
O	C	I	I	C	P	U	O	U	Q	E	W	A	L	V	P	M
A	B	A	B	T	E	G	C	M	B	U	N	Q	L	U	O	G
D	D	H	L	I	K	E	S	M	O	B	S	T	R	K	O	S
R	V	L	O	G	G	E	R	W	J	M	C	U	E	A	S	B
A	N	X	J	Z	N	U	F	L	C	S	G	R	B	T	X	J
W	S	R	W	T	K	O	O	B	K	O	O	L	I	E	N	A
M	L	O	S	U	V	W	X	A	F	E	K	H	I	B	U	I
Y	E	H	O	D	G	V	G	I	Y	D	Y	E	X	L	E	U
L	N	G	C	X	A	Z	Z	G	A	I	R	X	S	X	F	R
I	N	M	B	O	A	Q	V	N	I	V	E	B	O	M	H	S
F	A	R	V	J	F	T	K	S	R	E	M	A	G	E	I	D
E	H	M	Z	Y	J	T	L	A	T	B	J	R	N	M	O	F
U	C	A	R	U	M	T	Q	T	F	X	G	I	R	G	G	R
V	B	D	C	G	J	N	E	R	R	G	L	A	Y	N	O	I
H	V	E	Q	D	P	G	F	Z	S	D	N	K	O	I	B	W
Y	X	Q	Q	A	A	W	K	O	O	A	E	D	S	A	R	N
J	T	X	W	S	N	P	F	U	A	Z	N	V	R	X	K	D
R	T	U	H	P	F	D	M	K	Y	E	E	I	B	W	M	S
D	Z	I	A	I	G	Q	A	C	R	H	S	E	J	Y	Z	H
A	O	O	B	E	J	I	E	T	D	R	W	W	I	M	I	A
N	L	R	T	O	B	P	A	E	A	G	B	S	K	R	P	J

Sprinkle of Glitter

TOP ACHIEVEMENTS
Having her own book 'Life with a Sprinkle of Glitter' published as well as her diary range. Designing her own clothing line. Being a fab mummy to Darcy.

MOST COMPASSIONATE AWARD!
Louise has often spoken out about losing her mum at a young age. Since then she's gone and done some amazing stuff for charity, including dying her hair PINK for Cancer Research UK. With a tidal wave of support behind her she's raised almost £30,000 in sponsorship so far! Proud of you, Lou!

Name: Louise Alexandra Pentland
DOB: 28/04/1985
Family: One half-sister called Tiyana and a daughter called Darcy.
Pets: Two cats. They're brother and sister and are called Rocket and Zula.
Likes: Things that sparkle and spending quality mummy and daughter time with Darcy.
Dislikes: Sports. Bullying.
Single or Taken? Taken

/sprinkleofglitter
@sprinkleofglitr
@SprinkleofGlitr

BIO

Louise Pentland is a bubbly and brilliant blogger and vlogger from Northampton, UK. She was born on 28th April 1985 and is a proud mum to the world's cutest little girl called Darcy, or baby glitter as we also know her!

Louise's mega-successful career began when she started a blog that was based around crafting and lifestyle. This soon lead to her filming YouTube videos in 2010. Her following grew fast and as her army of Sprinklerinos expanded, she went on to start a second channel in 2012 where she vlogs about daily life and more personal content.

Louise is funny, down to earth and always totally up for some friendly banter. She's one of the coolest mum's we know and always has time for a smile and a kind word to anyone she meets. She basically just rocks at being an up-beat and awesome vlogger!

CRAZY CAT LADY!

Louise is totally obsessed with her two cats Rocket and Zula. OK, let's be real here, she's just totally obsessed with all cats! We reckon a perfect day in Sprinkle of Glitter land would definitely involve some furry feline friends!

DANCING DREAMS

Louise has made no secret of the fact that she is desperate to appear on the TV show Strictly Come Dancing. The hashtag #getlouiseonstrictly even trended on Twitter! You've got this Louise... one day!

YOUTUBE GURU

Louise won a YouTube Guru 'Shorty' award in 2016 crowning her as one of the best in the biz when it comes to beauty, positivity and style.

3 of the best

Louise or Zoe??

CHECK IT OUT

Prank Calls With Dan Howell

CHECK IT OUT

Draw my Life

CHECK IT OUT

YouTube channels

Main Channel – Sprinkle of Glitter
This is Louise's main channel where she posts crafting videos, beauty chat and general gossip. Yep, she's a total YouTube profesh! She has over 2,423,079 subscribers.

Vlogging Channel – Sprinkle of Chatter
This is where Louise uploads her vlogs and more chatty style videos. Over 1,094,686 'Sprinklerinos' have subscribed to this channel too!

The Epic Vlogger Quiz

Think you know everything there is to know about vloggers? Have a go at answering these questions and see how many you can get right!

1 Louise from Sprinkle of Glitter calls her viewers what?
a Chummys
b Cupcakes
c **Sprinklerinos** ✓

2 True or False:
Jim Chapman has a twin brother?

True

3 Which YouTuber has a brother in a famous band?
a Marcus Butler
b **Carrie Hope Fletcher** ✓
c Tanya Burr

4 The Saccone Joly family are originally from where?

Irland

5 Which of these titles is NOT a book by a YouTuber?
a **Me before you** ✓
b This book loves you
c Generation Next

6 True or False:
Joe Sugg AKA Thatcher Joe really did used to thatch peoples roofs for a living?

True

7 What is the name of Collette Ballinger's YouTube alter ego?

8 "Top of the morning to you laddies" is which YouTuber's catchphrase?

JackSepticeye

9 True or **False**: ✓
Before becoming YouTube famous, Alfie Deyes used to work in a bank.

False

Vlogger obsessed or a bit of a mess?! Add up your scores and see how well you did.

0-5 – OOPS!
With that kind of score, you'll be lucky to get any followers!

16

10 Zoe and Alfie live in which seaside location?
a St. Ives
b Weymouth
c Brighton ⟵ (circled)

11 Which of these two YouTubers have NEVER lived together?
a Jack Howard and Louise Pentland
b Dan Howell and Phil Lester
c Casper Lee and Joe Sugg

12 What is PewDiePie's real name?
Felix

13 Zoella was born in which month?
March

14 "Peace out, enjoy life and live the adventure" is which YouTuber's catchphrase?

15 With which YouTuber would you associate the documentary SNERVOUS?
a Troye Sivan
b Tyler Oakley
c KSI

16 Penny and Noah are characters from which YouTuber's book?
a Zoe Sugg ⟵ (circled)
b Carrie Hope Fletcher
c Sprinkle of Glitter

17 PewDiePie's girlfriend's YouTube name is?

18 **True or False:** Vlogger Casey Neistat lives in LA?

19 Tanya Burr is married to which fellow YouTuber?
a Joey Graceffa
b Jack Howard
c Jim Chapman ⟵ (circled)

20 Which of these is not a YouTube related event?
a SITC
b Insurgence
c Playlist Live

6-10 ROOM FOR IMPROVEMENT!
A good start but you should definitely swat up on your vlogger knowledge!

11-15 AWESOME!
Wow, great score. You're like a total pro at this!

16-20 OMG!
Move over Zalfie! There's a new star Vlogger in town!

17

MARCUS BUTLER

DID YOU KNOW?
I was part of a YouTube Boyband to raise money for Comic Relief?

RAPPING PRO
Marcus loves to release tongue in cheek rap videos. He even made it to number 85 in the UK charts with his hilarious video 'I'm Famous' featuring Connor Maynard.

Name: Marcus Lloyd Butler
DOB: 18th December 1991
Family: Two sisters Heidi and Natasha.
Pets: He had pet cats in his family home but has since moved out and no longer owns any pets.
Likes: Healthy food, going to the gym, listening to music, making people laugh.
Dislikes: Bullying or rudeness.
Single or Taken? Single
Catchphrase: "Heeeeellloooooo"

 @MarcusButler
 @marcusbutler
 /MarcusButlerTV
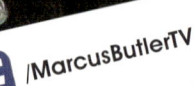 marcusbutler

BIO

Marcus Lloyd Butler was born on the 18th December 1991. He shot to YouTube stardom after starting a channel in 2010 and collaborating with various well-known YouTubers. He's the most social guy on YouTube and is friends with some of the best in the industry.

He loves to make his viewers laugh and some of his most popular videos have been collabs with other YouTubers. He also regularly creates his own hilarious and original content that shows us all just how creative and uber-talented this guy really is.

Marcus was part of the epic 'YouTube Boyband' that helped raised money for Comic Relief and he's no stranger to doing TV appearances after appearing on Ant and Dec's Saturday Night Takeaway show alongside fellow YouTuber Alfie Deyes.

He's always positive and upbeat but never holds back when he has something important to say and that just makes us love him even more.

CELEB PALS ANT & DEC

Marcus and Alfie recently starred on Ant and Dec's TV show 'Saturday Night Takeaway' so we imagine they must be pretty good pals with the Geordie duo by now, right?

THE HEALTH FOOD KING!

Marcus has always been really into his healthy eating. He's even started up his own business called Sourced Box – a healthy food subscription box.

SPORTS OBSESSED

Marcus loves sports and takes up any opportunity to get out there and be active. From ski-trips to snowboarding and just about anything that involves being fit and healthy.

AUTHOR ALERT!

Marcus made his fans even more obsessed by releasing his book 'hello life!' in November 2015.

3 of the best

The Official YouTube Boyband

CHECK IT OUT

Try Not To Laugh | Marcus and Niomi

CHECK IT OUT

120 Chicken Nuggets in 20 Minutes

CHECK IT OUT

YouTube channels

Main Channel – MarcusButlerTV
This is where Marcus posts his main channel content. It's a mix of funny content, pranks and collabs.

Vlogging Channel – MoreMarcus
You'll find more crazy content from Marcus including his daily vlogs.

Gaming Channel – MarcusButlerGame
All of your fave games as played by Marcus and his fellow YouTubers.

19

Spot the Difference

Take a look at the pictures below and put your eagle eyed vlogger skills to the test. Can you spot the 8 differences between picture A and picture B? Only a true vlogger fanatic will be able to work these out! Are you up for the challenge?....

JIM CHAPMAN

TOP ACHIEVEMENTS
Raising money for charity with the 'Internet Boy-band' – Releasing his own stationery range – getting a job as a writer for men's fashion mag GQ.

THE BRAINY ONE!
Jim is a total clever clogs. He graduated from the University of East Anglia with a degree in Psychology. #studygoals!

Name: James Alfred Chapman (that's 'Jim' to us!)
DOB: 28th December 1987
Family: A twin brother called John and two sisters – Sam and Nic from make-up channel PixiWoo.
Pets: The cutest little Dachshund called Martha.
Likes: Keeping fit, anything to do with fashion, modelling, spending time with his wife and family.
Dislikes: Internet trolls...erm... bellybuttons? What the heck, Jim!
Single or Taken? Married to fellow YouTuber Tanya Burr.

@JimChapman
@jimchapman
/OfficialJimChapman
jimchapman

BIO

Jim Chapman was born in Norwich. He first started his YouTube channel in 2010. Given that his sisters Sam and Nic from PixiWoo are practically vlogging royalty, it must have seemed like the next logical step for Jim!

Jim has been in a relationship with the super-talented YouTube sensation Tanya Burr since 2007 and the two tied the knot in September 2015, finally becoming husband and wife. Move over Brad and Angelina, there's a new 'power couple' in town!

Jim's YouTube channel has grown over the years and has seen him go from vlogging pro, to TV presenter and writer extraordinaire. He's hosted movie premières, written articles for some of the top fashion magazines and it seems like there's no stopping him now! Watch this space, because Jim is set to smash more of his targets this year and we can't wait to see him succeed.

ARTISTIC TALENT!

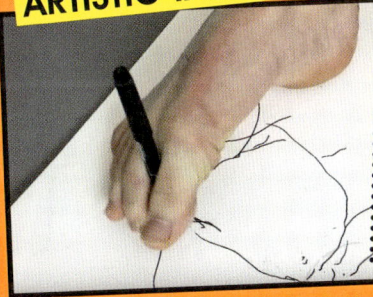

Jim is great at art. He's made loads of videos showcasing his talent and has even uploaded videos of himself drawing portraits with his FEET. Eww, kinda gross Jim, but we still love ya!

FAMOUS FAMILY

Jim isn't the only vlogger in his family. His sisters are Sam and Nic from the hugely successful PixiWoo beauty channel. His wife is beauty vlogger Tanya Burr and his twin brother (John) is also co-owner of TheLeanMachines a fitness and health based channel on YouTube. Keeping the YouTube talent firmly in the family there, Jim!

PERFECT PET

Jim and Tanya have a super cute puppy called Martha. She's a Miniature Dachshund who just loves the limelight. Martha's even got her own celebrity pooch pal in the form of 'Nala' - Alfie and Zoe's little pet Pug. These two get on just as well as their owners do and are definitely the best of friends. Cuteness overload!

3 of the best

Joe Sugg Waxed My Armpits

CHECK IT OUT

Jim and Tanya Mr and Mrs Challenge

CHECK IT OUT

Draw my Life

CHECK IT OUT

 YouTube channels

Main Channel – Jim Chapman
This is where Jim posts his main channel content. A mix of collabs, #AskJim and general fun.

Vlogging Channel – EveryDayJim
This is where Jim posts his vlogs. Follow him around London and beyond!

HARRY POTTER OBSESSED
Tanya is obsessed with Harry Potter. She wishes Hogwarts was real and that she was young enough to attend!

BEAUTY QUEEN!
Tanya has her own line of cosmetics. From nail polishes to false lashes, she's done it all!

FEARS & PHOBIAS
We all have things we don't like. Tanya apparently doesn't like the dark and is also scared of small spaces. She hates the dentist too. It's OK though Tan, those are all perfectly understandable!

BEAUTY QUEEN! Tanya Burr

Name: Tanya Burr
DOB: 09/06/1989
Siblings: A sister called Natasha and a brother called Oscar.
Pets: The cutest little Dachshund called Martha.
Likes: Creating new beauty tutorials and supporting worthwhile causes.
Dislikes: Scary movies, seeing people being unkind to others, small spaces – she's a little bit claustrophobic. Poor Tan!
Single or Taken? Married to fellow YouTuber Jim Chapman.
Top talent: Tanya plays the piano and even has one at home to practise on.

@TanyaBurr
@tanyaburr
/OfficialTanyaBurr/
tanyaburr

BIO

Tanya worked on a cosmetics counter before starting her YouTube channel in October 2009. Her decision to film videos was possibly inspired by spending so much time around the already successful PixiWoo girls, who just so happen to be her husband Jim Chapman's sisters! If you're going to learn, then learn from the best!

Tanya soon began uploading stylish and on-trend 'get the look' videos and celebrity make-up tutorials and her channel quickly took the internet by storm!

Her down-to-earth nature and her laid back filming style made her just like the big sister we could all totally turn to for beauty tips. With a friendly and positive nature she was soon getting subscribers from all over the world.

She gave us all a serious case of cuteness overload when she married fellow YouTuber Jim Chapman in September 2015 and the two seem totally smitten. Go team #Janya! She's currently got her sights set on new goals and is even taking acting lessons. Maybe this means we'll see Tanya Burr on the big screen someday?!

3 of the best

3 Minute Makeup Challenge!

CHECK IT OUT

Tanya Burr Vs. Jim Chapman Relationship Test

CHECK IT OUT

Baking Christmas Cookies With Joe

CHECK IT OUT

THE MUSICAL ONE!
Tanya loves to play music. She has a piano in her house and enjoys learning new songs. Is there no end to this gal's talents?!

TV SHOW OBSESSED

Tanya loves watching TV shows and some of her absolute favourites are The Vampire Diaries and Pretty Little Liars. We definitely approve of Tan's TV choices!

FAMOUS FRIENDS
Tanya Burr is popular with all of her fellow YouTube celebs. Some of her besties include Troye Sivan and Zalfie. She's even met loads of celebs! Most recently she posed for a cheeky Insta snap with none other than Kylie Jenner. #goals!

GLOBAL GOALS
193 world leaders are committing to 17 sustainable development goals, aiming to end poverty, fight inequality and tackle climate change over the next 15 years. In order to help achieve this, Global Goals are aiming to make all 17 goals famous, so they're not forgotten. Tanya Burr has become an ambassador and is hoping to help spread the word.
Find out more: www.globalgoals.org

YouTube channels
Main Channel – Tanya Burr
Tanya just has the one YouTube channel. She's totally keeping it simple and we're fine with that! This is the little corner of the internet where Tanya posts all of her main channel content, top videos and exciting announcements!

EDUCATIONAL FUN

YouTube is great for fun and games, but it's also a place where you can learn some pretty cool stuff too! These vloggers show that learning doesn't have to be hard work and that you can actually pick up some pretty cool tips and tricks!

CHECK THEM OUT

JACKSGAP

JacksGap channel is run by twins Jackson Frayn "Jack" Harries and Finnegan Frayn "Finn" Harries. Their channel was created by Jack while he took a gap year before starting his degree. Finn soon joined him and the channel blew the Internet's minds with their fun travel adventures and positive outlook on life!

4,227,523 Subscribers

CHECK THEM OUT

THE SLOW-MO GUYS

The Slow Mo Guys is a science and technology entertainment channel featuring Gavin Free and Daniel Gruchy. This mega popular channel shows loads of things being filmed in extreme slow motion using super-techy high-speed cameras. Now that's cool!

7,716,686 Subscribers

WORTH A WATCH:

4 videos from educational vloggers that are definitely worth checking out!

1. 6ft Man in 6ft Giant Water Balloon
2. Our Changing Climate
3. What if everyone jumped at once?
4. Immovable object vs Unstoppable force

- In the early days, Vsauce was one of the fastest growing YouTube channels back in 2012.

- The Slow Mo Guys were nominated for a Webby Award in 2016 – that's an award that recognises excellence on the internet!

- JacksGap twin Finn is older than Jack..... but only by 2 minutes!

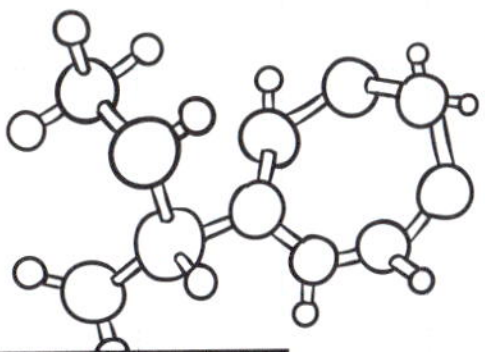

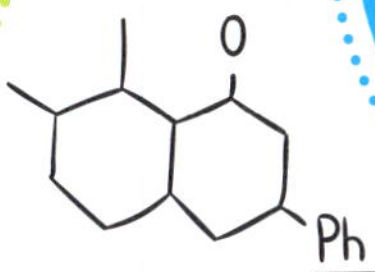

- Finn may have moved to New York City to study Design and Architecture for three and a half years but he is still a massive part of JacksGap!

- As well as MinutePhysics, there's also a MinuteEarth channel featuring physical properties and phenomena that occur on earth.

- In 2014 and 2015, Vsauce won a Streamy Award for Best Science and Education Channel.

CHECK HIM OUT

MINUTE PHYSICS

Created by Henry Reich, these easy to follow videos explain physics related topics in a matter of minutes! This means you get tons of knowledge in handy bite-sized chunks that you can watch with barely any effort at all. This is one channel that we think your teacher would be happy for you to watch after school!

3,298,080 Subscribers

CHECK HIM OUT

VSAUCE

Vsauce features internet personality Michael Stevens and features videos with scientific and philosophical themes, plus gaming, technology and culture. Some of the most popular videos have been 'What if everyone jumped at once' and 'Is your red the same as my red?'. There's never a dull moment on the Vsauce channel!

10,327,456 Subscribers

Can you list 4 things that educational vloggers have taught you?
Maybe you'll be surprised at just how much attention you've been paying without even realising!

1. ....
2. ....
3. ....
4. ....

FUN FOR LOUIS

YOUTUBER FAVE!
Louis is a firm fave with all of the top YouTubers. He counts Zoe and Alfie, Marcus Butler, Casey Neistat, Steve Booker, Dave Erasmus and many more, as some of his great vlogging buddies.

Name: Louis John Cole
DOB: 28/04/1983
Family: Two sisters – Darcy and Hilary.
Pets: Louis spends so much time on the road we're not sure he has time to look after pets!
Likes: Travelling the world, helping charities, meeting new people, coffee and of course, FOOD!
Dislikes: Being hungry!
Single or Taken? Dating fellow YouTuber Raya Encheva.
Catchphrase: "Peace out, enjoy life and live the adventure"

@FunForLouis
@funforlouis
/FunForLouis

BIO

Louis Cole is a daily travel vlogger from Surrey, England. He is currently living the dream and gets to spend his life travelling around the world with his friends. Yep, it really is as epic as it sounds!

He's always hopping on a plane to some far off place visiting new countries and destinations every week. Louis has friends all around the world and is well known and respected on the YouTube scene due to his laid back and down to earth personality. He's currently dating fellow vlogger Raya Encheva and these two seem totally on each-others wavelength. They both love to travel and are always looking for new and exciting places to explore together.

This guy has a crazy infectious energy that will make you want to save up your money and plan a holiday somewhere absolutely insane!

3 of the best

Draw My Life
CHECK IT OUT

Epic Paragliding 360 Video
CHECK IT OUT

Epic World Adventure
CHECK IT OUT

WHERE IT ALL BEGAN
At 16 years old, Louis and his best friend borrowed his parents car and randomly drove to Paris instead of going to school. Say whaaaat?! This is where Louis love of spontaneous travel and adventure was definitely born!

BEFORE YOUTUBE!
Louis and fellow YouTuber Dave Erasmus set up something called the 'Solvey Project' to help fund 7 individuals business ideas. They've travelled around the world listening to people's inspiring suggestions. What a cool project!

THE BOOM BUS!
Cole bought and completely renovated a double-decker bus, turning it into a mobile centre to help the homeless. It's decked it out with music and videogame facilities. It went on to be a great success and has helped loads of people. Nice one, Louis!

 **YouTube channels**

Main Channel – Fun For Louis
Daily travel vlogs and collaborations with his YouTuber pals.

FOOD FANATIC!
Louis is obsessed with food! He loves trying new food and drink in the various countries he visits and even used to have a whole channel dedicated to food called Food For Louis. It's rare we'll see a video from Louis that doesn't feature some tasty snacks along the way!

29

TOP ACHIEVEMENT

I've starred as Eponine on stage in Les Miserables.

THE LITTLE PRINCESS TRUST

Carrie's trademark blonde curls have made her instantly recognisable. She took drastic measures for The Little Princess Trust and had her hair chopped ridiculously short to raise money for charity. She's raised over £16,000 so far. Carrie, you're a star!

Carrie Hope Fletcher

ITSWAYPASTMYBEDTIME

Name: Carrie Hope Fletcher
DOB: 22nd October 1992
Siblings: A brother called Tom Fletcher. You might've heard of him. He's a bit famous!
Pets: She says she'll have lots of pets when she's got a bigger house and has settled down.
Likes: Spreading kindness and positivity, friends and family, bright colours and DISNEY, obviously!
Dislikes: Bullies!!
Single or Taken? She's dating fellow YouTuber Pete Bucknall and they might just be the cutest couple on the planet!

/ItsWayPastMyBedTime
carriehopefletcher
@CarrieHFletcher

BIO

Carrie Hope Fletcher comes from South Harrow in London. She's a mega-talented singer, actress and performer and has gained a huge following thanks to her positive attitude and kind nature. She's the 'honorary big sister' to the internet and since starting her channel in 2011 she's gone on to do some totally amazing things!

Carrie has been in successful theatre shows and still finds time to make YouTube videos and vlogs. She's starred in Les Miserables, War of the Worlds, Chitty Chitty Bang Bang and loads more.

Musical talent definitely runs in the Fletcher family. Carrie's brother is Tom Fletcher from McFly. Between the two of them, we reckon that they've got this whole vlogging thing sorted.

REAL LIFE DISNEY PRINCESS!

Carrie is a HUGE Disney fan. She has a soft spot for Stitch (from Lilo and Stitch) in particular and has also made a cover of Disney's 'I See The Light' from the movie Tangled. It was performed perfectly by Carrie and her boyfriend Pete!

CHILDHOOD DREAM JOB

When she was younger, Carrie had a random idea that she wanted to be an archaeologist. She's since realised that it might have just been because she loved the movie Indiana Jones!

CELEB PALS

Being in the public eye herself and having a famous brother means that Carrie has quite a few celeb pals. She counts Jason Donovan, Shane Ward and The Vamps as just a few of them!

AUTHOR ALERT!

Carrie has written her own book 'All I Know Now: Wonderings and Reflections on Growing Up Gracefully' and even went on to write a fiction novel called 'On The Other Side' shortly after that. Talented much?!

3 of the best

Taking Over Tom's House

CHECK IT OUT

Love is Easy With The Vamps

CHECK IT OUT

Pitch Perfect Cup Song Mashup

CHECK IT OUT

YouTube channels

Main Channel – ItsWayPastMyBedtime
This is where you can catch up with the latest from Carrie and watch her most popular uploads.

Second Channel – TwentyThirtyTwo
She may not use it quite as much but there are still a few gems to check out on this channel.

MATCH THE VLOGGER with the fact

Are you an encyclopedia of pointless YouTuber knowledge? See if you can match the vlogger with the fact!

Fact 1
"Before I became YouTube famous, I played competitive badminton and travelled all over the country for tournaments."

Who?
....

Fact 2
"We voiced a couple of cheeky seagull characters for The Spongebob Movie: Sponge Out of Water in 2015."

Who?
Joe and Casper

Fact 3
"The smell of mushrooms cooking makes me want to throw up!"

Who?
....

DAN HOWELL | MARCUS BUTLER | CARRIE HOPE FLETCHER | JOE SUGG & CASPER LEE | PEWDIEPIE | JACKSGAP

Fact 4
"I'm a successful vlogger but I also own the social media platform Beme."

Who?
....

Fact 5
"I once starred in a TV advert for a well known insurance comparison company."

Who?
....

Fact 6
"Our channel was originally started when we decided to take a gap year and travel before pursuing a degree."

Who?
....

Fact 7
"At the age of 13 I shaved my head completely bald for charity."

Who?
Tyler

Fact 8
"I once worked part time at a hot-dog stand to help support the early days of my YouTube career."

Who?
....

Fact 9
"In 2013 I raised $29,000 for my birthday in support of the Trevor Project charity."

Who?
....

Fact 10
"I gave up a career in Law to make YouTube videos!"

Who?
....

Fact 11
"In 2016 I cut off loads of my trademark curly hair to raise money for The Little Princess Trust."

Who?
....

Fact 12
"Before becoming a vlogger I did gymnastics for 10 years."

Who?
Alfie

Think you got them all correct? Check out the answers on the back page to see how well you did.

OLI WHITE · CASEY NEISTAT · ZOELLA · TYLER OAKLEY · PHIL LESTER · ALFIE DEYES

TOM FLETCHER

GEEK CHIC
Tom is the undisputed king of 'Geek chic' he wears what he wants, when he wants and looks great! He's obsessed with classic movies like 'Back to the Future' and loves comic books so his fashion choices usually reflect this. Go Tom, you're definitely super stylish!

DID YOU KNOW?
Because he sometimes has to remove his wedding ring when he's playing guitar, Tom decided to do something special for his wife Giovanna. He only went and had the initial 'G' tattooed on his wedding ring finger didn't he?! That's seriously awesome!

Name: Thomas Michael Fetcher (that's 'Tom' to us!)
DOB: 17th July 1985
Family: Tom's sister is Carrie Hope Fletcher. He's married to Giovanna Fletcher who also has a YouTube channel. Tom and Giovanna have two son's Buzz and Buddy Fletcher.
Likes: Song-writing, writing books, family time and being the best dad ever to Buzz and Buddy.
Dislikes: Public speaking.
Single or Taken? Married to Giovanna Fletcher.

@TomFletcher tomfletcher /officialtomfletcher

BIO

Tom Fletcher grew up in Harrow, London. He attended the Sylvia Young Theatre School and it was here where Tom met his wife Giovanna when he was just 13 years old. They've been together ever since. Cuteness overload!

He's been in the bands McFly and McBusted and has written songs for loads of different famous artists including One Direction, The Vamps and 5SOS.

Tom now lives with his wife and children and has turned his attention to making YouTube videos in his spare time. These have become insanely popular after his 'wedding speech' video went viral and has lead to his channel being featured on some of the world's top websites and news networks.

His sister Carrie Hope Fletcher is also a popular YouTuber and must have given him some cool tips to help him get started. That's what sister's are for though, right?

3 of the best

My Wedding Speech

CHECK IT OUT

Buzz and the Dandelions

CHECK IT OUT

Bump to Buzz

CHECK IT OUT

SUPER DAD!

Tom loves being a dad and it seems as though his parenting skills haven't gone unnoticed. In 2014 he won Marvel Celebrity Dad of the Year!

DEAR CARRIE!
Tom and his sister Carrie use their YouTube accounts as kind of an online diary. They make regular 'Dear Carrie' and 'Dear Tom' videos and we get to tune in and catch up with all of their latest gossip! Possibly the best diary ever!

AUTHOR ALERT!
Tom loves to write. He's penned a series of 'The Dinosaur That Pooped' books with bandmate Dougie Poynter and has even written a Christmas themed book called The Christmasaurus!

FAMOUS FRIENDS
Tom has managed to bag himself a few celeb besties. He knows the 1D lads and even penned a song for them. DJ and presenter Fearne Cotton is also a close friend and came to his wedding.

YouTube channels

Main Channel – Tom Fletcher
Tom posts his awesome YouTube videos here and always comes up with the most fun and original content!

Rise of the Beauty Vloggers

Beauty based YouTube videos are growing! With everyone loving a good 'haul' video and GRWM (that's short for get ready with me if you hadn't already guessed) it's easy to see why we just can't get enough of beauty vloggers and all of their latest adventures!

SAMANTHA MARIA

Samantha or Sammi as she's better known, is a fashion graduate from London who is obsessed with style and beauty. She vlogs about her life, the events she's attended and places she's travelled to. Sammi also creates some pretty awesome hauls and GTL videos!

1,756,777 Subscribers

LILY PEBBLES

Lily is a London based beauty blogger, vlogger and content creator. She makes videos talking about her opinions on the latest beauty products and also uploads weekly vlogs about her life. She's always in the know when it comes to new releases and her channel is full of inspiration for stylish living!

375,975 Subscribers

WORTH A WATCH:

4 videos from beauty vloggers that are definitely worth checking out!

1. Meet Piglet, Fleur de Force's super cute dog!
2. Affordable beauty with Lily's Drugstore Beauty Starter Kit
3. InTheFrow's beauty hacks
4. Sammi's super easy winged eyeliner tutorial

Fun Facts:

Victoria, from InTheFrow, has become well known for her trademark hair colour. But did you know that she's super brainy and has loads of qualifications including a Doctorate of Philosophy in the department of Textiles? So technically we can all refer to her as Dr Magrath!

Lily Pebbles is currently planning her wedding! She's gonna be the most stylish bride ever, right?!

Beauty vloggers get sent some of the coolest beauty products to test and review before they're even in the shops. How awesome is that?!

Most beauty vloggers don't just have a YouTube channel, they also have an online blog where they write up their thoughts. Anyone can start their own blog and you can even make one for free in some cases.

Fleur de Force is obsessed with her dog 'Piglet' but did you know that she also has two more dogs called Treacle and Squidge?

INTHEFROW

Victoria from InTheFrow, is always up to date with the latest in designer and high-street fashion and beauty. Her channel name literally means 'In the front row' and is a reference to sitting in the front row at the coolest fashion shows. She's stylish, fun and down to earth and we think she's fab!

473,697 Subscribers

FLEUR DE FORCE

Fleur is one of the best and most trusted names in beauty vlogging. She's been in it since the beginning and her videos are a mixture of tried and tested beauty, tutorials GTL and daily vlogs. She's got the cutest pets, including a Miniature Dachshund called Piglet!

1,367,811 Subscribers

Can you list 5 fashion or beauty products that you couldn't be without?
Whether it's your favourite pair of jeans, a new make-up product or a cool pair of trainers – jot down your faves below!

1. ....
2. ....
3. ....
4. ....

PewDiePie

TOP ACHIEVEMENTS

Wining a Shorty award for best Gamer in 2015. Having a whopping 43 Million subscribers to his channel!

PEWDS AND CHARITY

Felix, aka PewDiePie always makes sure that he works with as many charities as possible and raises money for loads of great causes. He's recently raised $153,000 in a campaign for clean drinking water around the world and over £342,000 for Save The Children. Bro fist coming right atcha, Pewds!

EVERYDAY LIFE

Despite being really loud and chatty in his videos, PewDiePie also enjoys the quiet life. He lives in Brighton and loves doing regular stuff like going to the movies with his girlfriend Marzia. Even Pewds needs some down time though, right?

Name: Felix Kjellberg
DOB: 24th October 1989
Siblings: One sister called Fanny.
Pets: Two super cute pugs called Maya and Edgar.
Likes: Gaming, horror movies and being creative.
Dislikes: Barrels.
Single or Taken? Taken. He's in a relationship with YouTuber CutiePie aka Marzia.

@pewdiepie
@pewdiepie
/PewDiePie

BIO

PewDiePie comes from in Gothenburg, Sweden. He was studying Industrial Economics and Technology Management before starting up his YouTube channel in 2010. His gaming videos soon grew in popularity and he began to realise that this was what he wanted to focus on full time.

Pewds grew a massive following which would soon be known as the 'Bro Army' a fan-base of loyal followers who tuned in every time he uploaded a cool new video. His content is based around gaming but he'll also make the occasional vlog too.

PewDiePie now lives in Brighton with his girlfriend, Italian YouTuber Marzia Bisognin and their two pugs, Edgar and Maya. Pewds and Marzia love to spend time together at home or travelling the world. With over 43 million YouTube subscribers, Pewds is the ultimate YouTube KING!

IN THE MEDIA!

Everyone knows the name PewDiePie and he's not just popular on YouTube. Pewds has appeared on TV shows such as South Park and has bagged interviews in some of the world's top magazines. Everyone wants a piece of him!

EDGAR AND MAYA

PewDiePie's pets have become celebs in his videos. They make regular appearances and it's clear that both Pewds and Marzia adore their fluffy little friends!

THIS BOOK LOVES YOU

In 2015 PewDiePie launched his own book. It is titled 'This Book Loves You' and it is filled with funny quotes and stories from Pewds himself. It's a must read!

KING OF YOUTUBE!

PewDiePie is the ultimate YouTube king! His channel has had over 10 billion views and he's one of the most subscribed to accounts on the whole of YouTube itself. His Bro Army is still going strong and his channel is growing day by day. How is this even possible?! He's just too cool...

3 of the best

Draw my life

Drawing YouTubers

Cream to the face challenge

YouTube channels

Main Channel – PewDiePie
This is where you'll find Pewds playing the latest video games and filming some crazy content for you bro's.

THE GAMERS

Gamers have some of the most watched channels on YouTube. They make great content and have created interactive and loyal fan followings. With the likes of PewDiePie, KSI and JackSepticEye making such awesome and hilarious content, it's easy to see why the gamers are raking in the views and the subscribers in record timings!

CHECK HIM OUT

CHECK HIM OUT

STAMPYLONGHEAD

Stampylonghead is a channel featuring a cute animated cat named Stampy Cat. Voiced by Joseph Garrett, this fun-filled channel is packed to bursting point with Minecraft themed videos and other awesome gaming content.

7,345,203 Subscribers

MARKIPLIER

Markiplier is American YouTuber Mark Edward Fischbach. He loves playing scary horror games and the Five Nights At Freddy's series is one of his most popular. He has loads of cool animated videos and his channel is fun, chatty and interactive.

12,636,611 Subscribers

WORTH A WATCH:

4 videos from Gamers that are definitely worth checking out!

1. Stampy's most popular video - Sinking Feeling
2. Markiplier 'Draw My Life'
3. Classic Ali-A - 'Worst Miss EVAR'
4. iHasCupquake Draw My Life

FUN FACTS :

- Markiplier was born on an air force base in O'ahu, Hawaii. He now lives in Los Angeles.

- Stampy's Lovely Book was published in October 2015 as part of a two book deal. The book is packed full of fun activities and jokes. Have you read it yet?

- Ali-A holds two Guinness World Records, for being the most subscribed COD channel and one for the most viewed COD Channel.

- iHasCupquake AKA Tiffany Michelle Herrera, competed in TV's Wipeout show and actually came fourth!

- Markiplier's older brother Thomas is a web comic author, and is behind the popular TwoKinds online comic.

CHECK HER OUT

iHASCUPQUAKE

Not all of the most popular gamers on YouTube are guys. In fact, there are loads of awesome girl gamer channels. iHasCupquake is one of the coolest girls on the YouTube block and she's known for her brightly coloured hair and her fun mix of gaming videos. Show em' how it's done Tiffany!

4,517,071 Subscribers

CHECK HIM OUT

ALi-A

Alastair Aiken, a popular British YouTuber who is best known for his totally awesome videos on The Call of Duty games. Ali-A is your guy for anything COD related. He covers the latest news In the run-up to new releases and uploads gameplay content. He also has a second channel Called MoreAliA where he uploads his Minecraft videos.

8,073,961 Subscribers

Can you list 45 games that you've played because YouTuber's have played them?
Make a note of your favourite video games below or jot down the ones that you really want to play next!

1.
2.
3.
4.

43

TYLER OAKLEY

TOP ACHIEVEMENTS
Releasing his book called 'Binge' - meeting Barack Obama and appearing on the Ellen show.

Name: Mathew Tyler Oakley (that's 'Tyler' to us!)
DOB: 22nd March 1989
Family: Tyler comes from a big family and has 12 brothers and sisters in total.
Likes: Disney movies, spreading kindness and positivity, helping charities.
Dislikes: Unkindness towards others.

@tyleroakley
@tyleroakley
/thetyleroakley
snaptyleroakley

BIO

Tyler Oakley's full name is Matthew Tyler Oakley but he began using his middle name Tyler when he was at school.

Tyler started on YouTube in 2007 and it began as a way to communicate with his friends while they were all studying at different universities.

Soon people began tuning in to his videos and Tyler realised that maybe he could turn YouTube into his career. Luckily for us, he began uploading more and more content and soon became one of the best known YouTubers ever!

CELEB PALS

Tyler has so many besties in the celebrity world that it's hard to keep up! He's friends with Darren Criss (GLEE) Ellen DeGeneres and has met and interviewed One Direction. We're totes jel, Tyler!

TV AND LIVE!

In 2014 Tyler had his own live show tour called "Tyler Oakley's Slumber Party". He's also got his own documentary called 'Snervous', so check it out if you wanna know the gossip behind Tyler's YouTube videos!

WRITTEN IN THE STARS

Tyler's star-sign is Aries. Aries personality traits are Spontaneous, Daring and Active to name a few. What do you think, does this sound like Tyler to you?

THE TREVOR PROJECT

Tyler is a long-time supporter of the charity The Trevor Project – an organization for the prevention of suicide in LGBT youth. He interned for them and continues to support them ever since. In 2013 Tyler raised $29,000 for his 24th birthday in support of the Trevor Project.

3 of the best

Draw my life
CHECK IT OUT

CHECK IT OUT
Tyler Oakley interviews One Direction

Tyler reacts to teens react to Tyler Oakley
CHECK IT OUT

YouTube channels

Main Channel – Tyler Oakley
The best place to keep up with Tyler's latest adventures! What's he been doing and who has he been hanging with this week?

Vlogging Channel – Extra Tyler
This channel isn't used by Tyler as much as his main channel but still has some pretty cool vlogs and additional content to binge watch!

THE TREVOR PROJECT
saving young lives

45

TOP ACHIEVEMENT

Releasing his first book, a graphic novel called Username Evie.

MR BRIGHTSIDE

Joe always seems to be happy and having a laugh! That cheeky grin of his seems to put everyone around him in awesome mood too!

THATCHER JOE

Name: Joseph Graham Sugg (that's 'Joe' to us!)
DOB: 8th September 1991
Family: He's the little brother of YouTube sensation Zoella.
Pets: Joe doesn't currently have any pets – maybe because he travels way too much!
Likes: Gaming, travelling the world with his mates, pranking Caspar Lee and doing funny impressions of people!
Dislikes: Not getting enough sleep, people crying and LOOM BANDS!

@Joe_Sugg
@joe_sugg
/ThatcherJoe

BIO

Joe grew up in Wiltshire, UK with his Mum, Dad and YouTuber sister – the one and only Zoella. Joe had a job thatching roofs and loved working outside, especially when the Great British weather was being ….. well... great!

After being regularly featured on Zoella's channel, Joe decided to start his own YouTube account. He soon became famous in his own right and began making video content that was creative and funny.

He's down to earth, doesn't take himself too seriously and just genuinely seems to be having a blast, totally embracing the course that his career has taken. Keep it up Joe – you're the best!

THE YOUTUBE BOYBAND!

Joe was one of the members of the 'YouTube Boyband' that raised money for Comic Relief. Well done for being such a good sport, Joe!

JOE AND CASPAR HIT THE ROAD!

Joe is great pals with fellow YouTuber Caspar Lee. The two of them even have their own DVD called 'Joe and Caspar hit the Road' where they travel around Europe working various different jobs. It's pretty cool!

VLOGGER FRIENDS!

Joe is friends with loads of his fellow vloggers. He used to live with Caspar Lee and is also great mates with Oli White, Louise Pentland (Sprinkle of Glitter) Tanya Burr and Jim Chapman! He's basically just everyone's fave guy!

CREATIVE TALENTS!

Joe is really keen on art. He loves creating his own pieces of artwork and even has plans to make his own art pieces for his London home.

3 of the best

My Sister Does My Makeup
CHECK IT OUT

More Amazing Impressions
CHECK IT OUT

Prank Calls With My Sister
CHECK IT OUT

YouTube channels

Main Channel – Thatcher Jo

Vlogging channel – ThatcherJoeVlogs
But shhhh he's not a daily vlogger - OK! ;)

Gaming Channel – ThatcherJoeGames
Where you can see what games Joe's loving right now!

47

Caspar Lee

DOING GOOD!
For my 21st birthday I wanted to raise £21,000 for the Comic Relief charity. I actually ended up raising over £23,000 for such an amazing cause!

TOP ACHIEVEMENTS
The publication of his book 'Caspar Lee' and raising loads of money for charity.

Name: Caspar Richard George Lee
DOB: 24th April 1994
Siblings: A sister called Theodora.
Likes: Travelling and hanging out with his fellow vlogging pal Joe Sugg.
Dislikes: Spicy foods. Remember the ghost chilli challenge?! Caspar also hates it when people spell his name wrong.

@Caspar_Lee
@caspar_lee
/casparlee

BIO

Caspar Lee was born in Paddington, London. He spent a lot of his early life living in Fort Nottingham, South Africa. He moved around a lot and lived in quite a few different places during his childhood.

When he was 16 Caspar started his first YouTube channel and travelled to the UK to collab with a few of his YouTube friends. He was having such a great time and decided that he wanted YouTube to be his full-time career!

He soon moved to the UK to live and his first room-mate was Alfie Deyes, who was also working on his own 'PointlessBlog' channel. Both began to get loads of subs and Caspar has since gone on to have some amazing adventures and capture them all on film for us.

We reckon he's only just getting started and can't wait to see what else Caspar Lee is going to get up to in the future!

3 of the best

New Apartment Tour
CHECK IT OUT

YouTuber Quiz with Zoella
CHECK IT OUT

Terrible Impressions ft Thacher Joe
CHECK IT OUT

STAR OF THE SCREEN!

Caspar featured as a character called Garlic the movie Spud 3: Learning to Fly. The movie also starred fellow YouTuber Troye Sivan! Caspar has also appeared in the Spongebob movie and in his own DVD 'Hit the Road' with Joe Sugg.

THE CASPAR LEE BOOK!

With so many YouTubers releasing their own books, Caspar wanted to do something a little different when he released one himself. He decided to release a self-titled book called 'Caspar', it's a biography that is actually written by his mum. She definitely knows him well enough to give us all of the gossip!

KING OF THE COLLABS!

Caspar loves a good collaboration video with other vlogging stars. In the past he's teamed up with the likes of Zoella, Oli White, Joe Sugg, Tyler Oakley, KSI and soooo many more!

YouTube channels

Main Channel – Caspar
This is where you'll find all of Caspar's top content!

Second Channel – More Caspar
Catch up with his vlogs, bloopers and extra content here!

49

DRAW my life

You've seen your favourite vloggers 'Draw My Life' videos and now it's your chance to get involved and draw your own! Use each of the spaces below to draw the best moments from your life, just like your favourite YouTube stars have done.

ME AND SOME OF MY BFF'S!
DRAW YOURSELF AND SOME OF YOUR BEST FRIENDS EVER!

WHEN I WAS LITTLE MY DREAM JOB WAS...
DRAW YOUR DREAM JOB!

ONE OF THE HAPPIEST DAYS EVER WAS WHEN...
DRAW ONE OF YOUR FAVOURITE DAYS THAT MADE YOU REALLY HAPPY!

Niomi Smart

TOP ACHIEVEMENTS
Running the London Marathon for Cancer Research UK. Having her own book 'Eat Smart' published.

MISS HEALTHY!
Niomi is the queen of healthy eating. She's always coming up with new recipe ideas and tips for eating food that tastes amazing but that's actually good for you too.

Name: Niomi Smart
DOB: 26th May 1992
Siblings: A little sister called Daisy May.
Likes: Healthy eating, exercising and cooking healthy and wholesome food. Making up new recipes.
Dislikes: We can't imagine that Niomi has many dislikes, she's always so happy and bubbly!
Single or Taken? She used to date YouTuber Marcus Butler but the two have since separated.

@niomismart
@niomismart
/NiomiSmart

3 of the best

BIO
Niomi Smart is a UK based YouTuber and blogger who is currently living in London. She first made her mark on the vlogging scene by appearing regularly on her now ex-boyfriend Marcus Butler's channel and everyone loved her!

Since then she decided to start her own YouTube account and has built a huge following of viewers who love the honest, positive and fun videos that she creates.

Niomi posts regular vlogs and also loves to update us all with her healthy outlook on life. She gives us all of the handy tips along the way of course!

Running the London Marathon 
CHECK IT OUT

Morning Routine
CHECK IT OUT

FASHION & STYLE!
Niomi might not be a fashion and beauty vlogger as such but she's got a great sense of style. She always looks good and seems to have her finger on the pulse of the hottest fashion trends.

Healthy snacks
CHECK IT OUT

VLOGGING BESTIES!
Niomi seems like a great friend to have. She gets on really well with Zoella, Tanya Burr and many more of her fellow vlogging pro's!

PUBLISHED AUTHOR!
Niomi loves cooking and creating recipes so much that she decided to write a book on it. Her book 'Eat Smart' is a play on her name and is packed with healthy recipes for every mealtime. We bet they're delicious!

NOT JUST A PRETTY FACE!
Niomi worked really hard at her studies and she actually has a LLB Law Degree! Go Nimbobs!

LONDON MARATHON!
Niomi ran the London Marathon in 2016 and raised over £3,000 for Cancer Research UK. That's our girl!

YouTube channels
Main Channel – Niomi Smart
This is where you'll find everything about Niomi. From her daily vlogs to her exercise tips and healthy recipes!

53

JACKSEPTICEYE

TOP ACHIEVEMENT
Reaching 10 million subscribers on YouTube!

SEPTIC EYE!
He called his channel "jacksepticeye" because when he was younger he was called Jack by his mum. The septiceye part comes from when he was at school playing football, a boy tried to head a ball at the same time as Jack. Jack got hit in the eye and he got a gross eye infection. True story!

Name: Seán William McLoughlin
DOB: 7th February 1990
Family: 2 brothers and 2 sisters.
Likes: Gaming, travel and meeting his fans.
Dislikes: Slow upload times!
Catchphrase: Top of the morning to you laddies!

@jack_septic_eye
@jacksepticeye
/officialjacksepticeye

3 of the best

BIO
Seán William McLoughlin aka jacksepticeye is an insanely popular gamer on YouTube. His awesome green hair and his cheeky personality have seen him become a YouTube sensation and we're not at all surprised!

The jacksepticeye channel first began to grow in September 2013 thanks to pro gaming YouTuber PewDiePie, who picked it as the winner of his "shout-out competition" for aspiring YouTubers with a modest number of subscribers.

At the time Jack's channel had around 2,000 subscribers compared to the 10 million he has now! He's put in loads of hard work and makes tonnes of great videos each week for us to check out. He's friendly, down-to-earth and it's clear that he genuinely appreciates all of his viewers support. We think he bloomin' well rocks!

THE MOST GRATEFUL TO HIS FANS!
As of 8 May 2016, he has 10,043,136 subscribers and 4,424,589,804 views. He was at pax when the channel hit 10,000,000 subs and made a video saying how grateful he was for all the support he gets from fans and friends. Aww, what a softie!

DEGREE!
jacksepticeye graduated high school with a degree in Music Technology.

HEAVY METAL!
Jack was a former drummer of indie heavy-metal band named Raised to the Ground.

IN THE BEGINNING!
His first ever video is a solid snake impression "war has changed" and the people who've watched his old videos will really notice the amount Jack has changed in the past few years!

TOP OF THE MORNING TO YOU LADDIES!
The jacksepticeye catchphrase that we all know and love was inspired by the character Monica Gellar in the TV show friends!

Draw My Life
CHECK IT OUT

Jacksepticeye Reacts To Adults React To Jacksepticeye
CHECK IT OUT

10,000,000 SUBSCRIBERS!
CHECK IT OUT

YouTube channels

Main Channel – jacksepticeye
This is where you'll find all of the amazing content from the one and only jacksepticeye. Tune in to see what games he's currently trying his hand at and what he's been getting up to!

55

Oli White

Name: Oliver White
DOB: 26th January 1995
Family: A younger brother called James.
Likes: Travel, spending time with his mates and his little brother.
Dislikes: Cactus plants!
Top achievements: Having his own book published called Generation Next.

 @OliWhiteTV
 @oliwhitetv
 /OliWhiteTV

BIO

Oli White is a British YouTuber born in Iver, Buckinghamshire. He's a funny, down to earth guy who has become well known on the vlogging scene due to his fun content and laid back personality. He's done lots of work outside of YouTube and has even tried his hand at presenting. Is there no end to his talents?

Oli is great friends with fellow vloggers Caspar Lee and Joe Sugg and these three often collab and travel to amazing places together. With Oli having just released his own book and his channel now growing even faster than ever, we think he's gonna be huge this year!

3 of the best

Brothers Play Pie face
CHECK IT OUT

YouTuber Olympics
CHECK IT OUT

You Called Me Prank
CHECK IT OUT

BADMINTON!
Oli used to play competitive badminton. He got so good at it that he was travelling all around the UK to play in tournaments. Go Oli!

THE CACTUS INCIDENT!
Oli got so sick of Joe Sugg's cactus related challenges whilst they were in LA that he actually filmed a video of himself eating a cactus. Are you crazy, Oli?!

OPPORTUNITY!
When he was just 17 Oli was hired by Guinness World Records to travel around the world and present 52 channels for their YouTube channel.

MMM DOUGHNUTS!!!
Talking about world records, in 2012, Oli set a new world record for eating a jam doughnut in the fastest time, without licking their lips!!! He did it in...wait for it...33 seconds. You are dough-nuts Oli, but we love ya!

YouTube channels

Main Channel – Oli White
This is where you'll find the most up to date main channel content from Oli.

Second Channel – Oli White Vlogs
Awesome vlogs from Oli!

Gaming Channel – Oli White Games
The best place to find out what Oli is playing right now.

57

Which VLOGGER are you like?

Have you ever thought that you've got the same personality traits as one of your favourite vloggers? Well here's your chance to take the quiz and find out which of these four awesome vloggers you're most like!

Q1 If you had a pet, what would you call it?

A. Simon
B. Nala
C. Edgar
D. Martha
E. GiGi

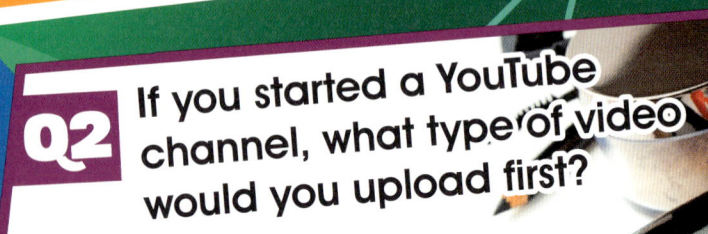

Q2 If you started a YouTube channel, what type of video would you upload first?

A. A beauty haul
B. A challenge video
C. A gaming video
D. A men's fashion haul
E. An NYC vlog

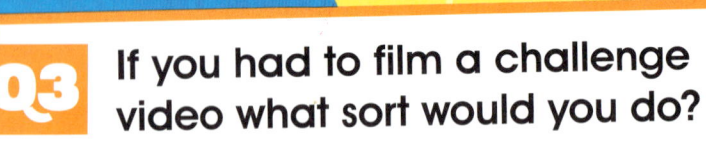

Q3 If you had to film a challenge video what sort would you do?

A. 7 Second Challenge
B. My Boyfriend does my make-up
C. Cinnamon challenge
D. What's in my mouth challenge
E. Race through the city on a boosted board.

Q4 What is your favourite food?

A. Pez
B. Pizza
C. Whatever!! Who has time for food when they're gaming?
D. A healthy smoothie
E. Candy

Q5 What would you prefer to be doing in your spare time?

A. Watching an awesome movie
B. Chilling at home with friends
C. Playing random games online
D. Having a pampering session
E. Making an awesome video with a drone

Q6 Who would be your YouTuber bestie?

A. Dan Howell
B. Louise (Sprinkle of Glitter)
C. Cinnamon Toast Ken
D. Marcus Butler
E. Jesse Wellens

Q7 If you could only visit one store, what would it be?

A. Forbidden Planet
B. Lush
C. Game
D. Top Man
E. Apple Store

Q8 What would your ideal game be?

A. Undertale
B. The Sims
C. Amnesia
D. Slither.io
E. I don't really have time for games anymore

Q9 What your biggest fear?

A. Bread crusts
B. Getting anxious in a crowded place
C. Barrels
D. Finding a grey hair
E. Not being productive

Q10 Which would your social media platform be?

A. Tumblr
B. Snapchat
C. Twitter
D. Instagram
E. Beme

So who are you?

Mostly A's
You are most like Phil Lester from Dan & Phil.

Mostly B's
You are the Queen of YouTube, Zoella.

Mostly C's
You are Swedish gaming legend Pewdiepie

Mostly D's
You are the suave and sophisticated all round good guy, Jim Chapman.

Mostly E's
you are the crazy cool New Yorker Casey Neistat.

PHIL LESTER

IT'S ALL IN A NAME

Phil's dad originally wanted to call him Richard or Jason but when he was born, Phil's mum thought he definitely looked more like a Philip. Phew, AmazingRichard just doesn't have the same ring to it!

TOP ACHIEVEMENTS

Voted 2013 Hottest Lad by Sugerscape. Created the character "Emo Goose" in Crossy Road and actually voiced it too.

Name: Philip Michael Lester
DOB: 30th January 1987
Siblings: Older brother called Martyn.
Pets: Phil used to have a pet shrimp called Simon, but it sadly died back in 2011, however Dan did buy him a plushie blobfish for Christmas.
Likes: Popcorn, the colour blue, Pokémon and Lions.
Dislikes: Cheese, as he is lactose intolerant and bread crusts – his Mum said they would make his hair curly and he didn't want that!!

/AmazingPhil
@amazingphil
@amazingphil

60

BIO

Phil was born in Rawtenstall, Lancashire in 1987. He's super intelligent and holds a degree in English language and linguistics as well as a Master of Arts in Video Post production. Totally techy!

Phil's first upload to YouTube was back in February 2006, but he's now made the video private (along with around 100 other uploads). His earliest available video is from March 2006.

Phil's main channel currently has around 3.5m subscribers and he gets loads of special guests onto his channel, including his house-mate Dan Howell which is hardly surprising as they've lived together since 2011!

SCREEN GIANT

Phil has appeared on our screens in lots of other ways apart from YouTube, He was a contestant on The Weakest Link, sat in the audience of Jeremy Kyle and also appeared in a TV advert. Phil has also been in a few films, the first one was Faintheart a 2008 romantic comedy, and more recently Phil and Dan voiced characters in the UK release of Big Hero 6.

RADIO

In 2012 The BBC gave Dan & Phil a crack at their own radio show. It was really popular and even won them the Sony Golden Headphones award for favourite radio presenters.

CHALLENGES

Phil has created some of the popular YouTube challenges, including the 7 second challenge. Dan & Phil even launched their own app – "The 7 Second Challenge"

RECORD BREAKER

In 2011, Phil won a Guinness World Record for fastest coin stacking by placing 25 coins on top of each other in 31.617 seconds.

3 of the best

Dan & Phil Punk Edits In Real Life
CHECK IT OUT

A Day In The Life Of Dan & Phil
CHECK IT OUT

Draw My Life
CHECK IT OUT

YouTube channels

Main Channel – AmazingPhil
Where Phil shares his awesome life with the internet.

Second Channel – LessAmazingPhil
More random goings on from the life of Phil.

Gaming Channel – DanAndPhilGAMES
Videos for Let's plays, reviews and challenges with the duo.

Arts & Crafts – DanAndPhilCRAFTS
OK, OK, this isn't really a channel, it was an April fools joke created by Dan and Phil – worth a look though for a laugh.

DAN HOWELL
danisnotonfire

POPULARITY ONLINE

Dan and Phil's gaming channel DanAndPhilGAMES reached 1 million subscribers within a year of its creation. That's insane!

STAR-SIGN

Dan's star-sign is Gemini. Gemini characteristics are: communicative, ready for fun, thoughtful, restless and indecisive. Does that sound like Dan to you?

Name: Daniel James Howell
DOB: 11th June 1991
Family: One younger brother.
Likes: Anime, socially awkward chats, food.
Dislikes: His so called 'Hobbit Hair'
Top achievements: Getting a gig as a Radio 1 DJ. Releasing 'The Amazing Book Is Not On Fire'.

@danisnotonfire
@danisnotonfire
/danisnotonfire

BIO

Dan Howell is one of the UK's best loved YouTube personalities. He was born in Wokingham, Berkshire and was actually about to embark on a high-flying career in Law before deciding to make a massive change and explore the world of YouTube instead!

Dan began uploading videos in 2009 after being encouraged by his friends. He loves nothing better than sharing his embarrassing life stories with us all and uploading content that we can totally relate to! He lives with fellow YouTuber Phil Lester (AmazingPhil!) and together they have done everything from presenting BBC Radio 1 shows to having their own book published. Awesome!

3 of the best

Dan and Phil react to Teens React to Dan and Phil
CHECK IT OUT

The Making of The Amazing Book Is Not On Fire
CHECK IT OUT

Dan and Phil Blindfolded Make-up Challenge
CHECK IT OUT

ON THE RADIO

Dan and Phil have joined forces on multiple occasions to present their own BBC Radio 1 shows, including their own show and regular appearances on 'The Internet Takeover Show' featuring loads of their vlogging pals!

CAREER FAILS

Dan has had some notoriously bad career fails that he's not been scared to document! These include getting fired from a DIY store after selling an axe to a 12 year old. No Dan, just no....

HELLO INTERNET

Dan's first video was called 'Hello internet' and he absolutely hates watching it now, because it makes him cringe! It's had over 2 million views though, so some people are still clearly loving it! Sorry Dan.

YouTube channels

Main Channel – danisnotonfire
Where you'll find all of Dan's main channel content and vlogs!

Second Channel – DandandPhilGAMES
Dan and Phil's awesome gaming channel!

VLOGGER BFF'S

Obviously Dan and Phil are total BFF's but Dan also gets on well with loads of other YouTubers. He's especially close with Louise (SprinkleOfGlitter) thanks to their shared awkwardness in public situations!

63

CASEY NEISTAT

TOP ACHIEVEMENTS
Launching 'Beme' and generally making awesome videos every day!

Name: Casey Neistat
DOB: 25th March 1981
Family: Casey has two brothers and one sister. He also has two children (Francine and Owen) and is married to Candice Pool.
Pets: A super sweet dog called GiGi.
Likes: Making movies and videos. Anything to do with technology and the latest filming gadgets.
Dislikes: Not having enough time in the day to get all of his cool stuff done!
Single or Taken? Married to jewellery designer Candice Pool.

MOST LIKELY TO....
Take his drone out to try and get some epic last minute footage for his vlog. Take a spur of the moment flight to an exciting destination. Give you the best film-making tips! Eat dollar pizza for breakfast and rush around NYC on his boosted board.

@CaseyNeistat
@caseyneistat
/cneistat

BIO

Casey Neistat was born in Connecticut. He had always wanted to make movies and loved the idea of being able to tell stories through video. After moving to New York he began to work on turning his dreams into reality and did everything he could to get the set-up he needed to start making his own movies. This included maxing out his credit card!

His determination paid of in the most epic of ways when he began getting paid work from companies and putting time into growing his own YouTube channel.

Casey's videos attracted loads of interest from the media and he soon had us all hooked on the daily vlogs from his New York City life. Casey always goes all out when it comes to his videos, he's creative, daring and constantly pushes the boundaries. Casey, you're one in a million!

SUNGLASSES

Casey's cool custom sunglasses have become kind of like his trademark look. He even showed how he made them in one of his videos so if you're curious, you can go take a look!

RESPECTED VLOGGER

Pretty much everyone on the vlogging scene has a crazy level of respect for Casey and his amazing ability to produce high quality and original videos. He's friends with the likes of PointlessBlog, Jesse Wellens, Karlie Kloss and loads more!

BEME

Casey likes to keep super-busy and has even found time to launch his own video sharing app called Beme. It's all set to be the next big thing - you've gotta check it out!

3 of the best

Snowboarding with the NYPD
CHECK IT OUT

Crazy German Water Park
CHECK IT OUT

What would you do with $25,000?
CHECK IT OUT

YouTube channels

Main Channel – Casey Neistat
This is where Casey posts his daily vlogs and newest content.

Casey Neistat's snapchat stories
These little videos were shot on Casey's mobile phone for Snapchat.

Casey Neistat classics
This channel is a place for all of Casey's old work. Some of the movies are just little scraps or fun things he did back in the day.

65

The Saccone-Jolys

TOP ACHIEVEMENT
I've starred as Eponine on stage in Les Miserables.

THE LITTLE PRINCESS TRUST
Carrie's trademark blonde curls have made her instantly recognisable. She took drastic measures for The Little Princess Trust and had her hair chopped ridiculously short to raise money for charity. She's raised over £16,000 so far. Carrie, you're a star!

Name: The Saccone-Joly Family
Family members: Jonathan, Anna, Eduardo and Emilia.
Pets: 6 Maltese dogs!
Likes: Pizza party Friday nights!
Dislikes: Spending time away from their family.
Top achievement: Winning a Shorty Award in 2016.

/JonathanPatrockJoly
/TheStyleDiet

@jonathanjoly
@annasaccone

@JonathanJoly
@AnnaSaccone

3 of the best

BIO
The Saccone-Joly family are an Irish family living in London. They vlog every single day and love sharing their daily life with their viewers. Jonathan was born in Ireland and his wife Anna was born in Baltimore United States. They're total vlogging pro's and the best parents too of course!

The Saccone-Joly's have been vlogging since 2009 and we've watched their little family grow right in front of our eyes. Anna and Jonathan have two children: Emilia and Eduardo. They also have 6 Maltese dogs – yes SIX!

PUPPY FRIENDS
Anna and Jonathan have 6 Maltese dogs. Their names are Albi, Sina, Theo, Bianca, Nivea and Nuvola. Albi actually only has one eye after a cat scratched him and left him badly wounded. He's not in any pain though and he looks just as cute as the rest of them. Shhh, you're our fave Albi!

ZALFIE BESTIES
The Saccone-Joly's and Zalfie are total BFF's. They always make time to catch up with each other whenever they can and of course, some of their hang-out time is filmed in their daily vlogs so you won't miss any of the fun!

JEWELLERY LINE
Anna actually designed her own jewellery line based on her Dad's necklace that she wears. The collection is zodiac themed and has been sooo popular. Proud of you Anna!

AWARD WINNERS
The Saccone-Joly's won a 2016 Shorty award in the Parent category. A well deserved win!

HOW THEY MET
Anna and Jonathan first met when Jonathan cast Anna in a music video he was directing. The rest…. is history!

Meet The Saccone Joly's
CHECK IT OUT

Zoella Is Our New Nanny
CHECK IT OUT

Toddler Meets Anna and Else in Disney World
CHECK IT OUT

YouTube channels
Main Channel – SACCONEJOLY's
This is where you'll find all of the Saccone-Joly's daily vlogs and their main channel content!

Jonathan's channel
Jonathan's own crazy content!

Anna's channel
Anna's own channel. Featuring 'What I Ate Wednesday' and more!

67

Find your VLOGGER NAME

Have you ever wondered what your vlogging superstar name could be? Use this super-easy chart below to work out what your superstar vlogging name is!

All you need now is some popular YouTube famous friends to hang out with and you'll be practically living the vlogging life, right?... erm, well...maybe.

HOW IT WORKS

Find the first letter of your first name in the chart and write it down (or remember) the name next to it. Then check the first letter of your surname, and do the same! Add the two names together and ta-dah! You've found your superstar vlogger name!

IF YOUR FIRST NAME BEGINS WITH...

THEN YOUR VLOGGING FIRST NAME IS...

A	Super
B	Wild
C	Awesome
D	Crazy
E	Uber
F	Incredible
G	Ultimate
H	(Amazing)
I	Funny
J	Mad
K	Sparkly
L	Rainbow
M	Wondrous
N	Smart
O	Fantastic
P	Glamorous
Q	Clumsy
R	Talented
S	Bored
T	Annoying
U	Grumpy
V	Unusual
W	Ranting
X	Ridiculous
Y	Stupid
Z	Childish

REAL NAME
Holly Williams

VLOGGER NAME
Amazing Reviwes

IF YOUR LAST NAME BEGINS WITH...

THEN YOUR VLOGGING SECOND NAME IS...

A	Sprinkles
B	Gamer
C	Fashion
D	Crafting
E	Vlogger
F	Cakes
G	Films
H	Stuff
I	Makeup
J	Rants
K	Comedy
L	Fun
M	Cats
N	Cooking
O	Jewellery
P	Clothes
Q	Shoes
R	Cities
S	Beauty
T	Memes
U	Music
V	Travel
W	(Reviews)
X	Advice
Y	Weather
Z	Art

How to be a Vlogging Pro

So you've seen all of your favourite vloggers making and uploading videos and maybe you've been thinking of having a go yourself? Take a look at some handy tips to help you get started.

Top Tips

Make Friends
Be social within the vlogging community or team up with friends who also like vlogging, it's fun to share your adventures!

Confidence
Everyone gets nervous at times, but try to be confident when you make your videos. There are people out there who really do care what you have to say, so be confident when using your platform!

Setting
Choose a good setting to film. Perhaps a quiet area of the house or somewhere clutter free where you can get your background looking just right!

Don't stress
Making videos should be fun! Don't sweat the little things and remember that it's OK not to take it all too seriously.

Work with what you have
You don't always need the fanciest of equipment or the most expensive camera. Use whatever you have to hand at first, some of the best vloggers started out with the bare basics and there's nothing wrong with that!

Plan Your Ideas
Find a nice notepad and jot down all of your ideas. This will be a great way to keep track of what you've already filmed and what you want to film in the future.

Everyone Starts Somewhere
You don't need to become an overnight success to make it as an awesome vlogger. Take your time and keep things simple at first, there's no rush! Even the biggest vloggers had to start somewhere...

Balance
Remember to spend some time away from your computer. Vlogging can be great fun but it doesn't have to take up all of your free time. Balance is definitely key!

Be Yourself
Don't feel like you have to change who you are just to make YouTube videos. Be yourself and have fun! If you are being natural and having fun, that will really come across on camera.

Comments and Social Media
Always use social media in a positive way. Why not leave a nice comment on someone's vlog today telling them what you enjoyed about it?

A - Z of Vlogging

A is for - Artistic: Being artistic and creative in your vlogs shows your passions and talents!

B is for - Branding: Design your channel art and social media banners to match your personality.

C is for - Camera: Learn what shots and angles look good by practising!

D is for - Daring: Dare to be different and don't always follow the crowd.

E is for - Energy: Put all of your energy and excitement into your vlogs!

F is for - Feedback: Listen to feedback from people around you.

G is for - Goals: Set yourself little targets.

H is for - Hard work: Put your time and effort into what you want to achieve.

I is for - Interact: Take the time to get to know other vloggers.

J is for - Judgement: Try not to judge what others are doing in their vlogs.

K is for - Kindness: Remember to be kind and considerate of others.

L is for - Laugh: Be prepared to laugh at yourself, even when you mess up in a video!

M is for - Memory Card: Make sure that you have enough space on your devices to film.

N is for - Notes: Keep track of anything important that you want to talk about on your channel.

O is for - Opportunities: Try to say yes to any cool opportunities that come your way on your vlogging adventure!

P is for - Personal Style: Have your own sense of style and don't let anyone change it.

Q is for - Q&A: A great way to let your viewers know more about you!

R is for - Roadtrips: Vlog your holiday or a day out!

S is for - Subscribers: Having loads of subscribers is cool but don't get too hung up on the numbers!

T is for - Teamwork: Why not collab with a fellow vlogger and make a new video?

U is for - Unboxing: If you're stuck for a video topic then these are always popular!

V is for - Vlog: The most fun hobby ever!

W is for - Waiting: Waiting for upload times will become the most annoying part of your day!

X is for - Xtra features: What else can you add to your vlogs that will make them more unique?

Y is for - YouTube: The coolest vlogging platform!

Z is for - Zalfie: Having a low moment? Think about how far Zoe and Alfie have come from their early vlogging days. Anything is possible, these guys are the proof!

Create your VLOGGING DOOR HANGER

Is some crucial vlogging activity taking place? Do you need the ultimate bit of peace and quiet to finish up your editing? Let people know that you're a V.I.V (That's Very Important Vlogger. Obvs!) by creating your own door hanger. Just follow the easy instructions below!

STEP 1
With scissors, carefully cut our both sides of the door hanger.

STEP 2
Put plenty of glue on the back of each door hanger.

STEP 3
Carefully stick both side together back-to-back.

STEP 4
Hang from the door handle of the room where you record your Vlogs!

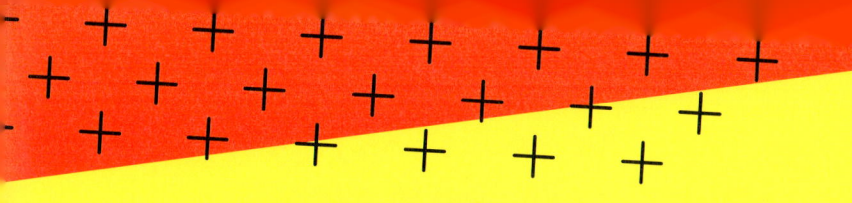

Side 1

VLOG EDITED AND UPLOADED

YOU CAN ENTER!

Side 2

V.I.V.

VERY IMPORTANT VLOGGER!

DO NOT DISTURB!

ONES TO WATCH

If you can't get enough of the top vloggers and are looking for some more to subscribe to then take a look at these awesome up-and-coming channels that we've found. You'll also find some exclusive quotes and tips from them! Trust us, they're gonna be huuuuge!

PetesJams

A fun-filled channel packed with stories, music and mayhem of the best kind! Pete Bucknall is fast becoming one of our most watched. He's funny, kind and just a really awesome dude!

PETE'S FAVES TO FILM: "I absolutely LOVE telling stories about things that have happened to me. I use a range of different voices, accents, and heaps of energy to create a world in which anyone can be drawn into, then leave feeling like they were actually there. And it has to be fun, ALWAYS fun. :)"

PETE'S ADVICE TO ANYONE THINKING ABOUT MAKING YOUTUBE VIDEOS: "YouTube is one of the best platforms for anyone to express themselves however they want to. It's a place that can help people's journey towards happiness. Use it to create and express yourself and do it in your own way. That's definitely the way to go."

Check this out!

I See the Light (Tangled Cover)
PetesJams and Carrie Hope Fletcher

@petesjams
@petesjams
petesjams

MegSays

A friendly women's lifestyle channel focusing on beauty, fashion, health and positivity.

MEG'S FAVES TO FILM: "I personally love filming 'monthly favourites' videos as I can make a cup of tea, sit down and have a nice long chat with my audience - I'm big on responding to comments so it's always lovely to find out what has been making them happy too! I also loved the process behind my '22 Things I've Learnt About Life in 22 Years' video as I pushed myself creatively, and it got a lovely reaction which I was over the moon about."

MEG'S ADVICE TO ANYONE THINKING ABOUT MAKING YOUTUBE VIDEOS: "If you can dream it, you can do it! It can seem daunting to put yourself out there but YouTube is, on the whole, a very fun, friendly and supportive place to express yourself and your ideas. There's room for everyone and if you've got something to share with the world, why not share it?"

@megsaystweet   @megsays   Meg Says

Check this out!
One Direction Live Lounge & Made In the A.M. Reaction

Emma Mumford

Emma Mumford is best known for helping people to save money. She's even known in the press as The Coupon Queen!

EMMA'S FAVES TO FILM: "My YouTube channel is full of beauty, lifestyle and savvy money-saving tips. I'm mostly known for being the UK's Coupon Queen, but wanted to show a more personal side of myself. I love doing monthly favourites and shopping hauls!"

EMMA'S ADVICE TO ANYONE THINKING ABOUT MAKING YOUTUBE VIDEOS: "Be patient, Rome wasn't built in a day and subscribers certainly don't appear out of nowhere. Make videos you enjoy filming, not what everyone else is doing!"

@couponqueenemma   @couponqueenemma   couponqueenemma

Check this out! Easter Egg Rocky Road Recipe

ANSWERS

12-13 Wordsearch

20-21 Spot the Difference

16-17 The Epic Vlogger Quiz

1. C
2. TRUE
3. B
4. Ireland
5. A
6. TRUE
7. Miranda Sings
8. JackSepticEye
9. FALSE
10. C
11. A
12. Felix Kjellberg
13. March
14. Fun For Louis
15. B
16. A
17. CutiePieMarzia
18. False
19. C
20. B

32-33 Match the Vlogger

FACT 1: Oli White
FACT 2: Joe Sugg and Caspar Lee
FACT 3: Zoella
FACT 4: Casaey Neistat
FACT 5: Phil Lester
FACT 6: JacksGap - Jack and Finn Harris

FACT 7: Alfie Deyes
FACT 8: PewDiePie
FACT 9: Tyler Oakley
FACT 10: Dan Howell
FACT 11: Carrie Hope Fletcher
FACt 12: Marcus Butler

36-37 Spot the Vlogger

PICTURE CREDITS

Little Brother Books Ltd would like to thank the following for their permission to reproduce their images:

Front cover:
Alfie Deyes © Ian West/Press Association Images
Louise Pentland © Ian West/Press Association Images
Marcus Butler © Vianney Le Caer/Invision/Press Association Images
PedDiePie © Jonas Ekstrmer/TT/TT News Agency/Press Association Images
Tanya Burr © John Phillips/Press Association Images
Zoella © Dominic Lipinski/Press Association Images

Back Cover:
Casper Lee, Tanya Burr & Joe Sugg © See Li/NewZulu/Press Association Images

(Key: t=top; b=bottom; c=centre; l=left; r=right; m=main;
page numbers referenced first; secondary numbers refer to the position of the image from the left)

Content:
Admedia/Zuma Press/ Press Association Images – 8; 33b7
David Jensen/EMPICS Entertainment/Press Association Images – 46; 39r
David Parry/Press Association Images – 35tl
David Sandison/Press Association Images – 9cl
Doug Peters/EMPICS Entertainment/PA Images – 6t; 30m; 32b3; 34; 56
Hannah McKay/ Press Association Images – 41bl
Ian West/Press Association Images – 22; 32b1; 62
Ian West/PA Wire/Press Association Images – 4l; 33b6; 48; 60
Joe Giddens/ Press Association Images – 35b
John Phillips/Press Association Images – 12r; 27r; 66; 68tl
Jonas Ekstrmer/TT/TT News Agency/Press Association Images – 32tl; 32b5; 40; 68b
Lauren Hurley/Press Association Images – 9tl
Matt Alexander/Press Association Images – 4r; 10; 21; 32tr; 33b4; 53l; 76br
Matt Crossick/Empics Entertainment/PA Images – 26l; 32b6; 33b1
Patrick Cashin/Press Association Images – 33b3; 64
Phillip Toscano/Press Association Images – 20
See Li/NewZulu/Press Association Images – 5r; 32b4; 23c; 52; 76tr
Sean Zanni/AP/Press Association Images – 6bl
Vianney Le Caer/Invision/Press Association Images – 14; 18; 24; 32b2; 53c3; 63b